To Marcel

The Bluffer's
Guide to
Philosophy

All Best!

IVM
3/24/95

The Bluffer's Guide to Philosophy

by T.V. Morris

Diamond Communications, Inc.
South Bend, Indiana
1989

**THE BLUFFER'S GUIDE
TO PHILOSOPHY**
Copyright © 1989 by
Diamond Communications, Inc.

*All rights reserved. No part of this book may be
used or reproduced in any manner whatsoever
without the written permission of the publisher.*

Manufactured in the United States of America

DIAMOND COMMUNICATIONS, INC.
POST OFFICE BOX 88
SOUTH BEND, INDIANA 46624
(219) 287-5008

Library of Congress
Cataloging-in-Publication Data

Morris, Thomas V.
    The bluffer's guide to philosophy.

    Bibliography: p.
    1. Philosophy--Humor. I. Title.
PN6231.P47M67 1989   102'.07   89-1414
ISBN 0-912083-35-2

"We always picture Plato and Aristotle wearing long academic gowns, but they were ordinary decent people like anyone else, who enjoyed having a laugh with their friends. And when they amused themselves by composing their *Laws* and *Politics* they did it for *fun*. It was the least serious and least philosophical part of their lives: the most philosophical part was living simply and without fuss."

—Pascal

ABOUT THE AUTHOR

T.V. Morris is a philosopher and a popular lecturer at the University of Notre Dame. He is the author of a number of other, *reputable*, books and of numerous professional essays which have appeared in nearly all of the leading philosophical journals. He is also an accomplished rock musician, a biographical fact completely irrelevant in the present context, but one which he insisted be mentioned. He is married and is the proud father of two young children who will be happy to see that he has finally managed to publish a book *with pictures*.

A NOTE ON THE ILLUSTRATIONS

The drawings were all done by the author, typically in free moments after too many cups of coffee, and thus with a shaky hand. The medium was magic marker, so what can you expect?

ACKNOWLEDGMENTS

I wish to thank all my colleagues who read earlier drafts of this guide, who corrected various of my mistakes, and who supplied a few of the lesser known stories contained herein. Any remaining errors, I lay at their doorsteps, since they are supposed to be experts. I wish also to thank Professor R. Kane, a philosopher at the University of Texas, or perhaps, more appropriately, his parents, for the existence of a name which contributed to inspiring this collection of arcane trivia and stories about the great philosophers. I would be remiss not to mention also in this connection the names of Professors S.O. Teric, Ab Struse, and Sue Donimus. And this book would be very different if it were not for my research assistants N.E. Fishant and M. Precise. Finally, I thank my wife, who was able to support me every step of the way, largely because she had no idea what I was doing.

CONTENTS

V. Twentieth Century Philosophy

INTRODUCTION TO PHILOSOPHY
BLUFFING: HOW TO USE THIS BOOK

It's time to face facts: On the contemporary social-cultural-intellectual scene, philosophy has become a *hot* topic. After decades of desuetude and obscurity outside the outermost periphery of the American consciousness, philosophy, of all things, is now definitely *in*. The former U.S. Secretary of Education, Wild Bill Bennett, is a philosopher. The man on the cover of a recent *Esquire* magazine who was described as having spearheaded the recent American Renaissance in stand-up comedy, Steve Martin, is known to have been a philosophy major in college, a fact often taken to explain in part his brilliant success with absurdity. One of the most popular contemporary American filmmakers, Woody Allen, loads his pictures with philosophical ideas. One after another, it is being revealed that numerous television and film personalities, martial arts experts, popular rock musicians, celebrity lawyers, and contemporary journalists have had a surprising amount of philosophy in their backgrounds, or secretly pursue the love of wisdom in their spare time. It is no longer just an isolated personality, like Jerry Mathers, "the Beave" in *Leave it to Beaver* (an early celebrity philosophy major); this is now a pervasive phenomenon. Philosophy has caught the attention of at least many of the leaders and role models of mainstream America. How else can we explain the fact that a book of philosophical argument, written by a professor of philosophy, has recently been perched atop the *New York Times* Best-seller List *for months*? The popularity of Allan Bloom's *The Closing of the American Mind* has served notice that Americans *want to philosophize*. But not everyone is equally well prepared to do so.

Recently while browsing through the Philosophy section of a local bookstore, I came across a book chapter entitled "Philosophy in the Conversation of Mankind." I was immediately reminded of a Yale undergraduate who once remarked to me after class: "Philosophy professors tend to get *so* abstract and go into *so* much detail. Don't they realize that most of us take philosophy courses just so, if sometime in the future, someone at a cocktail party mentions Plato or Aristotle, we'll know what they're talking about?" Whether we philosophers like it or not, that's the extent to which philosophy most often enters into "the Conversation of Mankind" nowadays. [1]

So what do you do if you find yourself in such a conversation, and you haven't had the requisite preparation at Yale or Notre Dame, or any similar institution of higher learning? If you're like many people who get into such situations, you may try to bluff your way out. But a knowing look and a nod of the head can get you only so far. It is amazing, however, what the knowledge of a couple of famous philosophical ideas and a good anecdote can do to secure for you a position of acceptance, and even prestige, in the eyes of others, who in most cases are no more than bluffers themselves.

This little book will provide all the basics for bluffing your way through the history of philosophy. You'll find entries for all the most important ancient, medieval, and modern philosophers—at least, for all those whose names are most likely to come up in typical bluffing contexts. The short profiles provided are a bit like what you might expect to see in an issue of *People Magazine* devoted to the great philosophers of history. Names, dates (in the only form most of us remember, centuries), nationalities, most important ideas, and biographical anecdotes are presented. When the name of a philosopher is tricky to pronounce, or easily could be mispronounced by someone merely seeing it in print, pronunciation information is given. Nothing undermines an otherwise promising bluff like the gross mispronunciation of a name (e.g. "Socrates" as "So-crayts"). Famous Latin phrases expressing ideas for which certain philosophers are renowned are also given. Nothing enhances a bluff like a bit of well-placed Latin. But correct pronunciation is important here too. A mispronounced Latin philosophy phrase may be recognized by a physician across the room as the technical name for a certain gall bladder or pancreas problem. The results could be unpleasant. But not to worry—classical Latin and medieval Latin differ a bit in pronunciation. Pronounce your phrases confidently enough and nearly any listener will assume you're doing so correctly ("It's the thirteenth century Paris pronunciation"). Appropriate pictures of the great philosophers are provided throughout this book, a carefully designed Appendix is also attached to further enhance your philosophical wit, and a useful Bluffer's Bibliography is given at the end to round out our collection and extend its usefulness.

You've never had a college course in the history of philosophy? Do not despair. This book offers you a chance to catch up with those who have, and even to get ahead of the game. You see, most people who have had the privilege of such a course tend to remember, a couple of years later, no more than two or three percent of what they were taught. That two or three percent is what you get in its purest form in this little book. But better than that, you get interesting stories typically known only to graduate students or professors of philosophy, fascinating facts that until now have usually been available only in the course of serious and time consuming scholarly research. Within these pages, they are yours for the asking.

Of course, there are two ways to bluff, intellectually speaking. Some pretenders to knowledge engage in the despicable and dangerous practice of uttering statements they have no reason to believe true, hoping to impress their hearers with their apparent display of knowledge. This is the stab-in-the-dark strategy. For the bluff to work, the hearers must assume, upon hearing them, (1) that the statements are true, and (2) that the speaker has reason to think they are true; that is to say, the speaker must be assumed to have been in the proper position to learn that of which he speaks (in prep school, at Yale or Notre Dame, or in independent, scholarly reading). The danger with this strategy is that a well-informed listener will spot the stab-in-the-dark, concocted statement as a falsehood, or will know enough to doubt its veracity and thus will almost certainly call the speaker's bluff by inquiring into the particulars of his sources ("where did you hear of such a thing?"—the bluffer's nightmare). This sort of bluff is despicable as well as dangerous because it is utterly careless about the truth.

The second way to bluff is to utter, as casually as possible, and at just the right conversational junctures, some fairly impressive statements you *do* have reason to believe to be true, and which are, typically, sufficiently esoteric that it will be assumed you could not have known the content of what they report without having had a rather impressive background of intellectual experience and attainment, a background which, as a matter of fact you do not have, since instead you picked up the tidbits in question from a source such as this book (a source you should of course *never* mention in the course of a successful bluff—if nonetheless you are asked the "Where did you learn this?" question, "in my reading" is a perfectly proper response). This, the short cut strategy, is probably the least despicable and least dangerous of all intellectual bluff strategies. It is not so very far removed from practices engaged in by many serious students of philosophy who, no matter how much they *do* know, always like to be thought of as knowing more than that. But it is a strategy which has been nearly unavailable to the layman until now.

There is, however, a problem here. Make the resources for successful bluffing widely enough available, and you make it more difficult for anyone to bluff successfully (upon hearing one of your knowing anecdotes, half your audience think to themselves "Oh yes, *The Bluffer's Guide to Philosophy*, page thirty"—bluff blown). But this doesn't worry me. The real purpose of this little book is to entertain you and, perhaps, to stimulate you to further reading in philosophy. The simple truth is, the more reading you do, the more interesting it becomes—and the more interesting *you* become. No bluff.

NOTE

1. For further witness to, and some dismay concerning, this Yale view of philosophy, see the memoir of another Yale graduate, Alvin Plantinga, in *Alvin Plantinga*, Profiles: An International Series on Contemporary Philosophers and Logicians, edited by James E. Tomberlin and Peter van Inwagen (Dordrecht, Holland: D. Reidel Publishing Company, 1985), pp. 20-21.

I.
Ancient Philosophy

The Pre-Socratics consider Thales' plight.

The Pre-Socratics

THE PRE-SOCRATICS ("pre-sock-ratics"; mainly 6th and 5th century B.C., Greek). A geographically and historically diverse bunch of guys, some with strange sounding names and even stranger sounding beliefs, these extraordinary early philosophers are most often just referred to *en masse*, and are known primarily just for beating Socrates to the punch. And it is an astounding fact that human beings that long ago, whose days were consumed in growing enough beans to consume, who lived so close to the edge of survival in nature, were able to begin reflecting on the nature of the cosmos in abstract ways. We're talking here about such thinkers as the "Annax boys": Anaximander, Anaximines, and Anaxagoras; the man who gave us the Four Elements, Mr. Earth, Wind, Fire and Water, Empedocles ("Empedocleez"), and the great-grand-daddy of atoms, Leucippus. It's worth saying a bit more about some of their fellows:

THALES ("Thayleez"; 6th century B.C., Greek). Thales believed that everything is made of water. His friends, of course, thought he was all wet. Appropriately enough, it is said that he once fell into a well and nearly drowned. Never one to let philosophizing make him too other-worldly, Thales became very rich when he was able to corner the olive market due to shrewd business dealing and an uncanny talent for agricultural predictions.

PYTHAGORAS ("Pie-thagerus"; 6th century B.C., Greek). This was a man who believed that all of reality is mathematical, that everything is ultimately composed of numbers. Notoriously, he also believed in the sinfulness of eating beans and in the transmigration of souls. A great mathematician who was revered by others, and had a famous theorem named after him, Pythagoras once stopped a man from beating a dog because he claimed he heard the voice of a departed friend in the yelping of the poor animal.

PARMENIDES ("Par-menideez"; 5th century B.C., Greek). Parmenides believed that nothing ever changes. And his opinion never did.

HERACLITUS ("...eye..."; 5th century B.C., Greek). Heraclitus disagreed with Parmenides, believing that everything always changes. He is known for his statement: "You cannot step twice into the same river." This memorable utterance was of course not meant to express a frustration about the prospects for riparian ambulation, but rather to give a vivid depiction of his altogether general view that, with respect to any kind of stuff, you cannot step into the same stuff twice, which makes it pretty obvious that neither he nor any of his pre-Socratic friends could have kept large pets in their yards. If my own experience at least is any guide here, it is quite possible to step into the same stuff more times than I would like to admit. But maybe in the days of open sandals, philosophers were just much more strongly habituated to caution in this regard. Our champion of change, by the way, was also known as "Heraclitus the Obscure," "The Riddler," and "The Weeping Philosopher."

DEMOCRITUS (late 5th, early 4th century B.C., Greek). Known as "The Laughing Philosopher," Democritus is famous for developing and promoting the view of his teacher Leucippus that everything is made of small, solid material atoms.

ZENO OF ELEA (5th century, Greek). This man was one of the first of the great thinkers to turn his attention to philosophical problems concerning space and time. Parmenides' star student, Zeno offered ingenious proofs that change and motion through space are impossible. To go from any point A to any other point B, you first have to travel half that distance. But to get to the halfway point, you first must travel half *that* distance, and so on, ad infinitum. But such an infinity of tasks can never be completed. Hence, no one can ever get where they're going (one of "Zeno's Paradoxes"). Unfortunately, we do not have access to the entirety of the clever man's philosophy. Before he could tell us the whole of his philosophy, he had to tell us the first half. But of course, before he could do this...

Socrates

SOCRATES (almost rhymes with "Opera tease"; 5th century B.C., Greek). (Easy trivia question: Who came first, Socrates or the Pre-Socratics?). Big city philosopher in Athens. Accused and convicted of corrupting the youth, his only real crime was that of having irritated a number of important people, although some say he had a criminally ugly face. Punishment: He had to drink the poison, hemlock. Famous quote: "The unexamined life is not worth living." But of course, it's also true that the unlived life is not worth examining. Socrates didn't write books; he just liked to ask probing and sometimes embarrassing questions which gave rise to the famous "Socratic Method" of teaching. This Greek philosopher made a career of deflating pompous windbags. Actually, he claimed he had been told by the oracle at Delphi that he was the wisest man in Athens. Seriously doubting this, he began questioning the citizens of the city to find someone wiser than himself. The surprising discovery: He was the wisest!—They all believed they had a wisdom they didn't have; Socrates was the only one who realized he knew nothing, and so he was the wisest after all. Or, at least, so he concluded.

Plato

LATO ("Play toe"; mid-5th century to mid-4th century B.C., Greek). An aristocratic man with plenty of money and a superb physique, Plato at one time won two prizes as a championship wrestler. Actually, the man's real (and little known) name was "Aristocles"; "Plato" was just a nickname given to him by his friends, a name whose original connotation made reference to his broad shoulders. He became an enthusiastic and talented student of Socrates, and wrote famous dialogues featuring his teacher verbally grappling with opponents. In one of his most notorious remarks, often repeated by women and barbarians with some measure of scorn, Plato said: "I thank God that I have been born a Greek and not a barbarian, a free man and not a slave, a man and not a woman; but above all that I have been born in the age of Socrates." Plato believed in the pre-existence and immortality of the soul, holding that life is nothing more than the imprisonment of the soul in a body. In addition to the physical world, there is a heavenly realm of greater reality consisting in Forms, Ideals or Ideas (such as Equality, Justice, Humanity, etc.). Well known image—"Plato's cave": Plato suggested that we are all like men shackled in a cave, staring at a wall, seeing only reflections and shadows and mistaking them for the real thing—the substantial realities are *outside* the cave, beyond what our senses can now show us. As his crowning achievement, he wrote a famous treatise on the ideal society, *The Republic*, in which he expressed the thought that it is a philosopher, of all people, who should be king (big surprise!).

Footnote to Plato:

"The safest general characterization of the European philosophical tradition is that it consists of a series of footnotes to Plato."
>—Alfred North Whitehead
>*Process and Reality*

"Oh yeah? Sez Who?"
>—Rejoinder falsely and
>anachronistically
>attributed to Aristotle

Aristotle

RISTOTLE (4th century B.C., Greek). Plato's best student, who went on to become the great tutor of Alexander the Great. Aristotle started his own philosophical school when he was 50 years old. He lived only ten more years, but amazingly produced nearly a thousand books and pamphlets, only a few of which have survived. Of course, we all know that the author of *Ecclesiastes* in the Old Testament speaks the truth when he says "the writing of many books is endless, and excessive devotion to books is wearying to the body." Aristotle knew this too, and so when he sat writing, he held a metal ball in one hand while he wrote with the other—when he became tired and began to nod off, the ball would drop to the floor and loudly awaken him back to philosophy. This great thinker was called a "peripatetic" philosopher (*peripateo* = "to walk around") because he liked to lecture to his students while taking a walk (another group of philosophers were called 'stoics' because they preferred sitting around on porches (stoa) when they shot the breeze). A key theme in his thought is that happiness (eudaimonia, pronounced "you day mow nee ah") is the goal of life. Aristotle was a good deal less other-worldly than Plato. He voluntarily went into exile from Athens when conditions became a bit politically dangerous for him, in his words, "lest Athens sin twice against philosophy" (see "Socrates"). The founder of logical theory, Aristotle believed that the greatest human endeavor is the use of reason in theoretical activity. One of his best known ideas was his conception of "The Golden Mean" - "avoid extremes", the counsel of moderation in all things. His famous student, the great and overachieving Alexander, obviously never got the point.

On Payment for Services Rendered:

"And so too, it seems, should one make a return to those with whom one has studied philosophy; for their worth cannot be measured against money and they can get no honor which will balance their services, but still it is perhaps enough, as it is with the gods and with one's parents, to give them what one can."*

—Aristotle

*Checks may be made payable to the author.

Diogenes the Cynic (just kidding).

Diogenes the Cynic

IOGENES THE CYNIC ("Dye-ah-janeez the sin-ick"; a.k.a. Diogenes of Sinope—not to be confused with Diogenes Laertius, Diogenes of Appolonia, or Diogenes of Ionoanda; contemporary of Aristotle, Greek). He was called a Cynic (from the Greek work *Kunikos*, meaning "doglike"), some say, because he looked like a stray dog. When the authorities in his unimpressive hometown condemned him to leave Sinope, he replied: "And I condemn you to stay in Sinope." Diogenes was well known for sometimes walking around in broad daylight, carrying a lighted lamp. Asked what he was doing, he responded: "Looking for an honest man." Two of his insightful sayings: "He has the most who is most content with the least," and "Dogs and philosophers do the greatest good, and get the least reward." The philosopher lived quite modestly in an earthen tub, with a few possessions—some say, with just a bowl for drinking water. But then one day he saw a slave boy drink with cupped hands and realized he could throw away the bowl. Surprisingly, Diogenes was Alexander the Great's favorite philosopher. Once Alexander went to see Diogenes. The following conversation ensued. Diogenes: "What, your Majesty, is your greatest desire at the present time?" Alexander: "To subjugate Greece." Diogenes: "And after you have subjugated Greece?" Alex: "I'll subjugate Asia Minor." Diogenes: "And after that?" Alex: "I'll subjugate the world." Diogenes: "And *then*?" Alex: "And then I plan to relax and enjoy myself." Diogenes: "Why not save yourself all the trouble by relaxing and enjoying yourself right now?" Standing over the philosopher, who was sunning himself at the time, Alexander asked before he left if there was anything, anything at all, he could do for him. Diogenes replied: "Get out of my sun." The sun-tanners' patriarch.

The Art of Refutation:

Having heard that Plato defined "man" as "a featherless biped," Diogenes plucked a rooster and said, "Here is Plato's man."

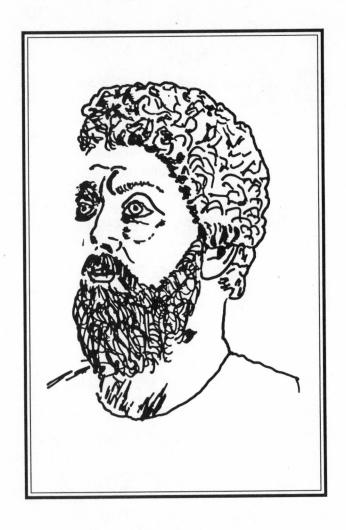

≡ *Marcus Aurelius* ≡

ARCUS AURELIUS ("Or-eelius"; 2nd century A.D., Roman). Roman Emperor and one of the two greatest Stoic philosophers. The other was Epictetus ("Epic-tee-tuss"), a Greek slave. It is said that they came to the Stoic philosophy of calmly accepting one's fate by two very different routes: Marcus Aurelius by his pessimism, Epictetus by his optimism. Marcus wrote aphorisms, short pithy sayings, while he was away on the military campaigns he so disliked. Typical stoic quote from Marcus: "Is your cucumber bitter? Throw it away." Also: "Do unsavory armpits and bad breath make you angry? What good will it do you? Given the mouth and armpits the man has got, that condition is bound to produce those odours." In light of the fact that the man of action was required to do so many things detestable to the man of thought, Marcus Aurelius' life has been described as the nightmare of a philosopher condemned to be a king.

II.
Medieval
Philosophy

St. Augustine

S T. AUGUSTINE (5th century A.D., North Africa). Bishop of Hippo. As a student, he managed to combine licentious living with academic excellence. Commenting on his habitual behavior, Augustine once said: "Frenzy gripped me and I surrendered myself entirely to lust." Never really seriously tempted by monogamy, he did live a while with one lover who bore him a child. In these early years, he admitted that he had devoted himself wholeheartedly to the pursuit of "promotion, profit, and praise." His mother Monica made it her life's goal to see him become a Christian. After many years of wild living and worldly success, he found himself very dissatisfied. During a difficult time, he was finally brought to Christian faith when he heard a young child at play say "Take and Read," "Take and Read." He took up St. Paul's letter to the Romans, read, and was converted. Within weeks of his baptism, her one life's goal accomplished, Monica died. Augustine went on to become one of the greatest of the Latin Church Fathers, although initially he didn't want to be a bishop; had to be dragged bodily, weeping, into the ordination. Two famous books: *Confessions* and *The City of God*. Well known quote: "Credo ut intelligam" ("I believe so that I may understand"). In later life, he recounted that along with a gang of other wild boys, he once stole some pears just for the perverse fun of it; due to this and his other many misadventures, he became convinced that humans are in pretty bad shape from sin and so depend strongly on God's grace for salvation. Augustine is remembered for his revealing prayer that God give him chastity—"but not yet."

APOCRYPHAL INTERLUDE

"Hey, what's that over there?"
"I can't see a thing."
"Who said that?"
"Over here."
"Where?"
"Here."
"Keep talking so I can find you."
"I've got nothing to say."
"Ouch! What was that?"
"Anybody got a darn light?"
"Who said that?"

> —Typical exchange among
> philosophers in the Dark Ages,
> following Augustine.

Boethius being consoled by philosophy.

≡ *Anicius Manlius* ≡ *Severinus Boethius*

NICIUS MANLIUS SEVERINUS BOETHIUS (just called "Bow-ee-thius" for short; 6th century, Roman). Christian, statesman, Platonist philosopher. Boethius has been called "the last of the Romans", and "a founder of the middle ages." Imprisoned on false charges, he claimed to be consoled by philosophy, and so he wrote a book called *The Consolation of Philosophy*, a book whose ideas went on to console such later thinkers and writers as Dante, Chaucer, Gibbon, and Pope. At the end of his imprisonment on false charges, he was executed. Boethius is known by many theologians for his famous definition of divine eternity ("the whole and complete possession of unending life"). He once characterized God as "a substance that is super-substantial," typical of the linguistic creativity at which philosophers are so accomplished.

St. Anselm

ST. ANSELM (11th century, Archbishop of Canterbury, England). Like Augustine (and, some say, Aristotle as well), Anselm as a young man gave himself up to temptation, and for a short time lived in a dissolute, profligate way, impoverishing himself to the point that he was once forced to eat snow to assuage his excessive hunger. But afterwards, again like Augustine, he came to lead a life of exemplary moral rectitude. A thinker from the beginning, he disliked thoroughly the administrative tasks he was assigned in the church as his talents were recognized. When chosen by the king to be Archbishop, he had to be carried bodily into the king's presence to receive his commission. He was, nonetheless, a great and legendary church leader. His biographer Eadamer tells us that he once healed a blind man, brought rain in a drought, prevented by his very presence a severely damaged ship from taking on water through a gaping hole, fell into a deep well and emerged unscathed, prayed surrounded by supernatural fire on at least one occasion, and successfully predicted on numerous occasions that a large fish of some specific kind would turn up, one way or another, to satisfy the needs of a hungry person. He is remembered primarily as the Father of Scholasticism (applying logic to theology). He thought of God as "that than which no greater can be conceived" or, the greatest conceivable being. Based on this idea, he also invented the most famous argument for the existence of God, the Ontological Argument, which has irritated atheists for centuries. The main contention of the argument is that from merely understanding the concept of God, we can prove that there is a God. Some commentators have thought it to be one of the greatest and most powerful arguments ever devised, while on the other end of the spectrum, critics such as Schopenhauer have dismissed it as merely a "charming joke."

News for both Thales and Anselm:
"Truth lies at the bottom of a well."
   —Diogenes

Peter Abelard

ETER ABELARD ("Abba-lard"; late 11th, early 12th century, French). Exceedingly strong, handsome and popular philosopher best known for seducing at the age of 39 one of his students, Heloise, the seventeen year old beautiful and talented niece of a powerful church canon at Notre Dame Cathedral. Said the philosopher: "Under cloak of study, we freely practiced love." In retribution, her uncle's friends performed a small but painful operation on Peter which left him with a lower weight and higher voice. Interestingly, one of his main contributions to metaphysics was a theory of personal identity as consisting in the retention through time of "principal parts." This theory led one critic, Roscelin, to question Abelard's own identity after the consequences of the Heloise misfortune.

Moses Maimonides

*M*OSES MAIMONIDES ("My monidees"; 12th century, Spanish born, Egyptian Jew). Widely known for coming up with one of the greatest philosophical book titles in history: *Guide for the Perplexed*. He is, however, not as well known for one of his other books on a common medical disorder which any sufferer of the malady sitting and pondering his plight must deem to be very appropriately titled: *On Hemorrhoids*. Nickname: Rambam. The multi-talented Maimonides was employed by the Sultan of Cairo as his personal physician. One day the Sultan complained to Maimonides that he had been paying him a sizable salary for quite some time, and yet had never been ill enough to make use of his services. At risk of losing his retainer, Maimonides quickly explained that that was precisely what he was being paid for—thereby introducing the Sultan to the novel concept of preventive medicine and insuring himself a continued income, in sickness and in health. The philosopher-physician also ran a busy hospital in Cairo. A medieval, type-A overachiever personality, he once explained his tardiness in answering a letter by writing that "I am working so hard every day, that in the evening when I receive private patients, it is I who am lying in bed and they who must stand."

Saint Thomas Aquinas

S T. THOMAS AQUINAS (13th century, Italian). A very, *very* fat Dominican, Aquinas was one of the heaviest thinkers at a time when the greatest minds were often housed in the largest, most corpulent bodies, a time not inappropriately known as the "middle" ages. Corroborating the medieval metaphysical principle that effects resemble their causes, his literary output is often described as "enormously voluminous". Aquinas was probably the single greatest Christian thinker of all time. One of his most famous contributions has come to be known as "The Five Ways": Five arguments for the existence of God; the most famous is known as the Cosmological Argument. Aquinas was definitely a late bloomer: his teachers and fellow students called him "the dumb ox." Only one teacher was perceptive enough to dissent from this opinion, Albert the Great. Said he: "You call him a Dumb Ox; I tell you that the Dumb Ox will bellow so loud that his bellowing will fill the world." When Aquinas first announced to his family that he wanted to become a simple friar, his brothers took him by force and locked him away in a castle. Once, as he was seated by the fire, they sent in a beautiful prostitute to lure him away from his religious intentions. It is reported that he chased her out of his cell with a hot poker.

John Duns Scotus

J OHN DUNS SCOTUS ("Scoe-tuss"; late 13th century, British at a time when, reportedly, the Irish were called "Scots", and the Scots were called "Irish".). A brilliant philosopher and extraordinarily gifted, charismatic teacher at Oxford and Paris. Because of the intricate arguments of which he was capable, he was known as "The Subtle Doctor" (philosopher St. Thomas Aquinas was called "The Angelic Doctor," and T.V. Morris, the author of this volume, must admit that friends and relatives who wanted him to go into medicine, where he could become a *real* doctor and make *real money*, sometimes refer to him, in reference to his Ph. D., as "The Phony Doctor"). Duns Scotus was known for his cutting Irish wit, which sometimes got him into trouble. Few historians, however, think he ever reached the pinnacle of dangerous repartee attributed to that earlier Scotus, John Scotus Erigena (9th century). Once Scotus Erigena was seated at dinner across the table from King Charles the Bald, a man often given to excessive drinking. Joking about Scotus' heritage, Charles said, "Tell me, John, what separates a Scot from a sot?" The Not-So Subtle Doctor immediately replied, "The width of the table, Sire." As is the case with many charismatic personalities, Scotus' students began to emulate him, to the best of their abilities. And as is too often the case, they were *very* poor copies of the master, perfecting his worst traits and missing altogether those qualities which made him great. Hardheadedly conservative and ponderously dull, they came to be known after his death as "Duns men," or "Dunces men," whence we derive the word "dunce."

Some Other Honorific Titles of the Middle Ages:

Alexander of Hales - "The Irrefragable Doctor"
St. Bonaventure - "The Seraphic Doctor"
Roger Bacon - "The Wondrous Doctor"
Richard of Middleton - "The Solid Doctor"
Raymond Lull - "The Illuminated Doctor"
Giles of Rome - "The Firmest Doctor"
Henry of Ghent - "The Solemn Doctor"

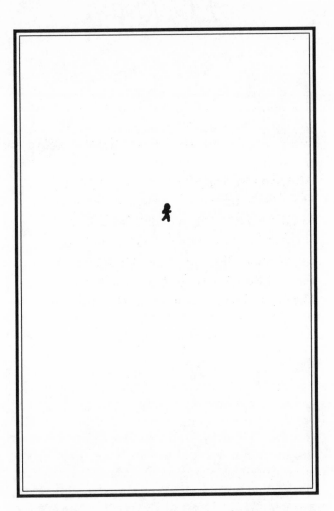

Ockham, viewed from a great distance.

William of Ockham

WLLIAM OF OCKHAM (Rhymes with "rock'em" or "sock'em", appropriately enough, since he was an intellectual fighter known as "The Invincible Doctor"; 14th century, English Franciscan). Decided that Universals (like Plato's Forms) don't exist, that they are just an unsightly outgrowth of metaphysical speculation. He shaved away this "Plato's beard" with "Ockham's Razor"—the metaphysical principle that says: Don't multiply postulated entities beyond necessity. He became infamous for the extreme claim that whatever God does is by definition good, regardless of what it is. He believed that there are no objective moral values apart from God's commands, and once even went so far as to say that "if God had commanded his creatures to hate Himself, hatred of God would have been praiseworthy." Ockham got into big trouble with the Pope for condemning some dubious policies of the Church. He expressed extreme disapproval of the enormous sums of money being lavished on a building being erected to honor St. Francis of Assisi, the founder of his own Order, and wrote a powerful "Defense of Poverty" opposing the Pope. He was jailed, escaped, and sought refuge with the Emperor of Germany, saying "You defend me by the sword and I will defend you by the pen." The result? He was excommunicated. Ockham has the enduring distinction of being the only great philosopher whose place of burial is marked by a plaque in a parking garage (in Munich, Germany). He is, however, more remembered for his logical acumen than for the distinctiveness of his eternal parking place.

APOCRYPHAL INTERLUDE
Great Minds on Toiletries:

Moses on hot combs - "No, no, no; it was a
burning *bush*, not a burning *brush*."

Anselm on pet grooming accessories - "I didn't
say that the early Christians used *cat combs*;
the word is *catacombs*."

Ockham on the razor - "I would much rather
have had a good after-shave named for me."

Agrippa on the tooth-brush - "First you get a
good Agrippa, and thena you brusha up and
down."

Mill on the floss - "The greatest dental care for
the greatest number!"

Dewey on evaluating cosmetics - "It's not easy to
compose a good make-up exam."

III.

Renaissance Philosophy

Actually, this is *not* Agrippa. But it's a
good guess as to what he looked like. It
is what someone else looked like, but
what's the difference?

Henrickus Cornelius Agrippa von Nettlesheim

ENRICKUS CORNELIUS AGRIPPA VON NETTLESHEIM ("On-reek-us...", called "Agrippa" for short; early 16th century, German, who travelled and worked throughout Europe). One of the great names of the Renaissance (not a particularly great thinker, just a great *name*—other great Renaissance names include Alexander of Aphrodisias, Giovanni Francesco Pico della Mirandola, Pietro Pomponazzi, Pietro Bembo, and Dionigi da Borgo San Sepulcro). He was a diplomat, a military man, an occult magician, a Catholic theologian and religious reformer, a medical doctor and a lawyer—in short, a standard Renaissance man. One of the *very* few philosophers of former times to have written on "the superiority and nobility of women," he is also known for his revelatory discovery that "philosophers disagree about everything."

IV.
Modern
Philosophy

= Francis Bacon =

FRANCIS BACON (late 16th, early 17th century, British). Founder of modern inductive scientific method. Sometimes described as "a philosopher who lived like a fool." Said to have been a greedy extortionist, he himself once announced, "I lean to Thales' opinion that a philosopher may be rich if he will" (see "The Pre-Socratics"). He married for money, and then, determined with a vengeance to "bring home the bacon," Francis fought and finagled his way rapidly up the social ladder, finally to become Lord Chancellor of England. Life in the fast lane came to an end when he was accused of, and investigated for, bribery. Protesting vigorously, he tried to stop the investigation by bribing the King. Famous quote: "A little philosophy inclineth a man's mind to atheism; but depth in philosophy bringeth men's minds about to religion." He died from a cold, which he caught while performing a refrigeration experiment—stuffing a chicken with snow. We may surmise that, in all likelihood, friends and bereaved relatives at the breakfast table, for a long time afterwards, would wince at any mention of "Bacon and eggs."

Thomas Hobbes

THOMAS HOBBES (17th century, British). Lived off wealthy patrons like many other philosophers of his time. He is especially famous for his writings in political philosophy. In fact, Hobbes had one of the longest literary careers in history: he published his first book at age 14, his last when he was 91. By far, his most famous book was the *Leviathan*. Hobbes thought that without governments to restrain people, the "state of nature" would be "a war of every man against every man." One of his best known quotes depicts "the life of man" in a natural state as "solitary, poor, nasty, brutish, and short." He was not known for positive thinking. Hobbes is considered by many to be the founding father of modern materialism (nothing exists but bodies, "corporeal things"). He even suggested that God is "a great corporeal spirit" (of especially *refined* matter, he went on to specify, thereby avoiding the criticism of some who mistakenly characterize his position as the view that, for all we know, God may be a fat man in Cleveland). Hobbes, it is well known, was not afraid to admit that he was afraid of nearly everything.

≡ Rene Descartes ≡

RENE DESCARTES ("Wren-ay day cart"; 17th century, French). Often called "the Father of Modern Philosophy," Descartes spent most of his life searching for a way to unify all of human knowledge; but in his last few years he was mostly captivated by the problem of how to keep his hair from turning gray. In the midst of his life of searching, he once declared that a beautiful woman, a good book, and a perfect preacher were, of all the things in the world, the most difficult to find. Descartes began his philosophical work with sceptical questioning in search of one indubitable truth to use as a foundation for all of knowledge. The truth? *"Cogito ergo sum"* (I think, therefore I am", originally expressed by him in French, not Latin, as *"Je pense, donc je suis"* - pronounced "zhay", "ponce", "swee"). That, and the conviction that "God is not a deceiver," helped him stop worrying that life is all a dream or a deception cooked up by an evil genius. For most of his life, he had a famous habit: he stayed in bed meditating every day "until midday." He then made the mistake of taking a position with the Queen of Sweden as her personal philosophy tutor, for which he was required to rise well before five each morning. He was dead within months. Descartes believed that humans have minds and experience, but animals don't. This is said to have led one of his followers to kick his own dog repeatedly in amazement that it could act so much like it was in pain when it didn't have a mind with which to feel pain.

APOCRYPHAL INTERLUDE
Last Entry from Descartes' Notebook:

I eat therefore I am - a good start, but it's too Epi-
curean sounding

I shave therefore I am - somehow reminds me
too much of Ockham

I love therefore I am - nice thought, but remember what happened to Abelard

I sneeze therefore I am - dubious, they'll never
buy it

I burp therefore I am - I can tell I need to take a
break

I sleep therefore I am - memorable, but even
shakier

I dream in living color therefore I am - keep it
simple, stupid

I think therefore I am - that's it!   Bull's eye!
Bingo, the *Cogito*: This is gonna make me famous, I can feel it.

Note to myself: Tomorrow - Remember to finish
this doggone sentence!   I think therefore I
am...*WHAT*?

Blaise Pascal

BLAISE PASCAL ("Blaze pass-call"; 17th century, French). Talented mathematician and scientist early in life. Famous quote: "The heart has reasons of which Reason knows nothing." Great books: *Pensées* ("pon-say"; actually, notes for a book he never finished but which were published posthumously, and have gone on to become in their own right a perennial best-seller). Famous mystical experience—"The night of fire." Pascal carried a memorial of this experience around with him everywhere, written on a piece of parchment, sewn into the lining of his coat. He contrasted "the god of the philosophers" with "the God of Abraham, Isaac, and Jacob." He is also renowned for developing a striking argument for betting on God, which has come to be known as "Pascal's Wager": If, in this life, you bet that there is a God and you win, you win an infinite reward—everlasting life; if you lose, you don't lose much. Whereas, if you bet against God (you act as if there is no God) and win, you win little; if you lose, you have lost big. So the most rational bet is to wager on God. Despite being a philosopher himself with such original ideas, Pascal often made fun of philosophers, especially Descartes. Once, he even offered this assessment of what too often passes for philosophy: "Even if it were true, we do not think that the whole of philosophy would be worth an hour's effort." Hence, the brevity of this book.

Benedictus Spinoza

ENEDICTUS (also Baruch, "Bar-ook") **SPINOZA** ("Spin-o-za"; 17th century, Jewish philosopher born in Amsterdam, Holland). A lens maker by trade, Spinoza's life involved a greater than usual number of noteworthy spectacles. Widely referred to as "the God-intoxicated man," for believing that God is an absolutely infinite being, and so identical with the whole of reality, he was banned from the synagogue, on the charge of *atheism*! An original thinker with many unorthodox views, he exercised prudent caution in letting his views be known only to a few friends, for his were times in which unorthodoxy was dangerous. He was, however, no coward, once facing down an angry crowd which had falsely accused him of being a spy, and on another occasion being locked in his own house by his landlord, who refused to let him confront a murderous, frenzied mob with his low opinion of their actions. Spinoza thought that all of human knowledge could be arranged according to the pattern of deductive science, such as Euclidean geometry—beginning from indubitable axioms we would deduce everything there is to be known. His major problem was that he could never quite manage to make his philosophical writings clear or easy to read. Nor were they well reviewed. Anticipating, and perhaps even surpassing, the tone of some contemporary philosophical book reviewers, one particular commentator described a book of his as "a wicked instrument forged in hell by a renegade Jew and the devil."

"Spinoza is the noblest and most lovable of the great philosophers. Intellectually, some others have surpassed him, but ethically he is supreme. As a consequence, he was considered, during his lifetime and for a century after his death, a man of appalling wickedness."

—Bertrand Russell

G.W. Leibniz

G.W. **LEIBNIZ** ("Lyebnits"; late 17th century, German). Believed that this is the best of all possible worlds, a belief ridiculed by Voltaire in his famous book *Candide* ("can-deed"). Leibniz is well known to have held the even more unusual belief that everything in the world is composed of small immaterial things called "monads" ("mo" pronounced like "go"; monads are said by Leibniz to "have no windows"). Leibniz also believed that nothing happens without "a sufficient reason" (the renowned "Principle of Sufficient Reason"). Whether the utterly general principle is true or not, we do know that Leibniz would at least never spend his money without completely sufficient reason. Whenever a young lady at the court of Hanover would marry, Leibniz would present her with a "wedding present" of useful advice, in the form of short maxims, culminating in the admonition not to give up bathing, now that she had landed a husband—not a particularly good way to build a reputation for liberality or good taste. There is a famous logical law named after him, and also an excellent imported butter cookie, available at finer grocery stores.

John Locke

JOHN LOCKE ("Lock"; 17th century, British). Founder of British Empiricism. Locke was a somewhat paranoid philosopher who nonetheless stressed the importance, in philosophy as well as in life, of common sense. He lived in Holland under the assumed name of "Dr. Vand de Linden" for about five years. As a young man, he read Descartes and disagreed with him on so many things that it spurred on his own philosophical development. He thought college was dull, but became a professor for a while anyway. Although he had not graduated with a degree in medicine, Locke nevertheless decided to set up a medical practice. After a frustrating evening of philosophical discussion with friends, he once decided to write an essay to clear up some disputed matters concerning the limits of human understanding. Writing it ended up taking twenty years. When it was published, it was formally condemned by the authorities at Oxford. Locke said that he took that to be "a recommendation of the book." Something of a late-bloomer, he published his first article at the age of 54. He is well known for having opposed the view held by others that we are born with innate ideas; he thought that all our ideas have to come from *experiences*. At birth, every human mind is a *tabula rasa* or blank slate, upon which experience will write. Of course, some just remain blanker than others.

George Berkeley

GEORGE BERKELEY ("Barklee"; 18th century, British). Famous quote: "*Esse est percipi*" ("*esse*" pronounced like "messy," per kipee; means "to exist is to be perceived")—nothing exists except spirits and the perceptions, or ideas, of spirits. When I leave the room, my desk would disappear unless God continued to perceive it. There is no such thing as matter existing apart from thought. In a famous attempt to refute Berkeley and to prove that matter *does* exist, Samuel Johnson once theatrically kicked a stone. The result? No refutation, just a sore toe. Took the draft of a major book with him on a long vacation; lost it on the trip and couldn't make himself rewrite it. At least, like many students of philosophy after him, he *claimed* to have written a major contribution and to have lost it. But he also claimed that tar water could cure almost any ailment. Berkeley was a man who loved to sit on the beach and philosophize. Moreover, it was his dream to establish a new center of civilization in the New World (the Americas) by founding a college of the first rank on the beautiful island of Bermuda, with easy access to the beach. The dream failed, however, through lack of sufficient funds (a common enough problem where Bermuda is concerned). A California university with fairly good access to the beach is named after him, although the pronunciation of the name has been Americanized. When the cornerstone for a college at Yale also named after him was laid on November 2, 1934, a passage from Berkeley's writings was read, while the stone itself was anointed with: tar water!

There was a young man who said, "God
Must think it exceedingly odd
 If he finds that this tree
 Continues to be
When there's no one about in the Quad."

   Reply

Dear Sir:
 Your astonishment's odd:
I am always about in the Quad.
 And that's why the tree
 Will continue to be,
Since observed by
    Yours faithfully,
    God

    —Ronald Knox

David Hume

DAVID HUME (18th century, Scottish). A real man-about-town (Edinburgh) and a famed historian, a popular guy and expert in backgammon. His French friends called him "*le bon David*." In Scotland friends called him "Saint David." He shared with many other philosophers a love of food, resulting in a pronounced corpulence. During an extended visit to Paris, where he was celebrated for twenty-six months as one of the world's greatest men, his favorite hostess was fond of calling him her "Fat Wag" and "Fat Rascal," names he greatly enjoyed. In France, Hume was much admired by the ladies, and plainly enjoyed it, saying on one occasion, "I retain a Relish for no kind of flattery but that which comes from the Ladies." Nevertheless, he was a bit awkward in matters pertaining to romance, or even the appearance thereof. He was once placed on a sofa between the two prettiest women in Paris for a parlor game in which he was to play the part of a sultan attempting to win the love of his two beautiful slaves. A witness reports that he could manage to do nothing but slap his knees and belly while saying repeatedly "Well, young ladies; well, there you are then! Well, there you are!," for a quarter of an hour. Finally, one of the ladies lost patience, got up and blurted out, "Ah! I expected as much; this man is good for nothing except to eat veal!"

Hume is known by philosophy students as one of "the British Empiricists." He wrote a number of well-received books, but complained about one of them which was ignored after publication that "it fell dead-born from the press." Hume never held an academic appointment, though twice he applied for a chair of philosophy. He conceived the idea for his greatest book, *A Treatise of Human Nature*, when he was 18, and completed it at age 26. He is well known for having given a famous argument against the reasonableness of ever believing on testimony that a miracle has occurred. He even went so far as to admit that he was a sceptic about nearly everything, *as long as* he was in his study. In reference to Hume's scepticism, his antagonistic contemporary, Dr. Samuel Johnson, commented to James Boswell, "Truth, Sir, is a cow that will yield such people no more milk, and so they are gone to milk the bull." Boswell himself had a higher view of the philosopher, and summed him up well, saying that "David Hume, who has thought as much as any man, who has been tortured on the metaphysical rack, who has walked the wilds of speculation, wisely and calmly concludes that the business of ordinary life is the proper employment of man." Registering his concern with truth, Hume once said, "A wise man ... proportions his belief to the evidence." He faced his own death from cancer, which he believed would be his annihilation, with cheerful philosophical acceptance.

"I was a man of mild disposition, of command of temper, of an open, social and cheerful humour, capable of attachment, but little susceptible of enmity, and of great moderation in all my passions. Even my love of literary fame, my ruling passion, never soured my temper, notwithstanding my frequent disappointments."

—David Hume
Self-obituary

Jean-Jacques Rousseau

EAN-JACQUES ROUSSEAU (pronounced a bit like "Shawn Shack Ruse-Oh", 18th century, French). Wrote on politics and philosophy of education. A philosophical chameleon, he changed his views, or at least expressed contradictory views, incessantly (He converted from Protestantism to Catholicism, back to Protestantism, etc., and would condemn the rich on one page of his writings only to condone and praise them a few pages later). Swiss by birth, Rousseau was a true celebrity of his time, entertained, promoted, and cared for by the munificent nobility of France, though neither his life nor writings merited much by way of celebration. His life provides ample corroboration of those regrettable pieces of sociological folk wisdom, "It's not what you know that counts but who you know," especially Counts, and "It's not what you say, but how you say it." The love that all of France seemed to have for him was surpassed only by that which he had for himself. Publicly thought of as the embodiment of virtue (He himself exclaimed: "Show me a better man than me!"), an intimate characterized him as "a moral dwarf on stilts"; known as the patron saint of romanticism, he was unbelievably calculating and selfish in relationships and, sexually, in the words of one biographer, most often seemed to prefer "taking matters into his own hands." A paranoid hypo-chondriac who often dictated his works from bed, he was terribly thin-skinned over the criti-cism of others: Once a woman he was trying to seduce with flowery, amorous talk broke into a fit of giggles and thus so upset him as to give him a hernia.

"Well, at any rate I shall get his clothes."

—Rousseau,
   consoling himself
   upon the death
   of a close servant.

Immanuel Kant

IMMANUEL KANT ('a' pronounced either of 2 ways: as in "father" or in "ant"; 18th century, German). Most famous Russian philosopher (in a sense—his hometown is *now* a part of the Soviet Union, but in the same sense a number of the Greek Pre-Socratics could now be claimed as Turks). As a young man and a student, he lived a life of poverty and deprivation. He often went hungry, but preserved his health by "breathing only through my nose in the winter and keeping the pneumonia winds out of my chest by refusing to enter into conversation with anyone." Barely five feet tall, he was to become one of the giants of philosophy. Reading Hume awakened him from his "dogmatic slumber." Best known book: *The Critique of Pure Reason*, sometimes described as a nearly unreadable masterpiece of philosophy. Kant himself described it as "dry, obscure, contrary to all ordinary ideas, and on top of that prolix." He was right. He once sent the completed manuscript to a friend, who was himself an eminent scholar. The man read some of the book but returned it unfinished, explaining "If I go on to the end, I am afraid I shall go mad." Born in Konigsberg, Prussia, Kant never left town. He took a walk every day with such regularity (at 3:30 in the afternoon), people could set their clocks by him. In his philosophical work, he tried to restrict reason to make room for faith. He believed that theoretical reason can't reach beyond the world of experience, and so he disliked the traditional "proofs" of the existence of God. He wanted instead to make religious belief a matter of "practical reason." Kant chose philosophy over marriage because of the slight medical problem of having appeared to have begun life more or less like Abelard ended it (See Peter Abelard). Famous distinction: the phenomenal world (things as they appear to us) vs. the noumenal world (things as they are in themselves). Famous conception of morality: acting on the motive of duty alone. His principle of universalizability in ethics is often alluded to by the common question: "What if everybody did it?" But to this, there is a common rejoinder: "They don't."

APOCRYPHAL INTERLUDE
Great Minds on Groceries:

Augustine on condiments - "All I said to
Pelagius was that, so far as I can tell, no one
can cut the mustard."

Bacon on lettuce and tomato - "A great combination!"

Descartes, when asked what was in the cup-
board (one of the most misquoted lines in history) - "I think there are four yams."

Kant's critique of pure raisins - "They make
me way too regular."

Sartre's Cheap Existential Diet - "Beans and
Nothingness."

═ *Jeremy Bentham* ═

EREMY BENTHAM (mid-18th to mid-19th century, British). Famous quote: "Nature has placed mankind under the governance of two sovereign masters, pain and pleasure." Our moral goal is to maximize the balance of pleasure over pain. Bentham developed a "hedonic calculus" to help in our deliberations. In his will, he left a great deal of money to his college, University College of the University of London, on the condition that they exercise whatever art of taxidermy or embalming might be required to preserve his dead body, clothed and sitting in a chair, holding his brain in a jar, and in addition that at the big college dinner *every year*, they bring him out and seat him at the head table before a full meal. The college accepted his condition, and his money. Whatever minor pain this has caused the diners at University College, the story has brought immense pleasure and delight to philosophy students everywhere year after year, in accordance with the requirements of his moral theory.

George Hegel

(GEORGE) W.F. HEGEL (Rhymes with "bagel"; late 18th, early 19th century, German). Harder to read than Kant. Thought by many to be only the second major philosopher after Socrates to be married (The first?—Berkeley). Also thought by many to be very confused. Interestingly, like his married British predecessor, Hegel was a famous Idealist philosopher: all that really exists must be mental, there isn't, ultimately, any independent material stuff. The history of the world is the history of the Absolute concretizing itself, and is a history of development (a "dialectical development" - one thing happens [a thesis], the opposite happens [its antithesis], and from a dynamic tension, a higher resolution [a synthesis] arises). Art and Religion are, like Science, forms of thought. The highest form of thought?—You guessed it, philosophy. On his deathbed Hegel complained, "Only one man ever understood me." He fell silent for a while and then added, "And he didn't understand me."

Arthur Schopenhauer

ARTHUR SCHOPENHAUER ("Show-pen-our"; 19th century, German). Philosopher of pessimism. Clear and elegant writer. He is notorious as a misogynist, a true hater of women, a personality trait created in him by his mother, a literary lady with immodest pretensions who began to dislike her precocious son when she once read that there could not be two geniuses in the same family. Schopenhauer once said of other recent philosophers that they "first exhausted the thinking power of their time with barbarous and mysterious speech, then scared it away from philosophy and brought the study into discredit." He was an extraordinarily fearful man who kept his purse under lock and key, always slept with a loaded pistol near him and took elaborate precautions to avoid any possible contact with any disease. He was also emphatic about doing his own shaving because, as he put it, "I wouldn't trust my neck to another man's razor." If nothing was alarming him, he grew alarmed at that very condition; for it is bad enough to be endangered, but worse yet to be endangered by something of which one is ignorant. He on one occasion declared that his three favorite characters in history were Buddha, Kant, and his own pet poodle. Said Schopenhauer: "I feel most at home among demigods and dogs. They alone are free from the failings of men."

Ludwig Feuerbach

LUDWIG **FEUERBACH** ("Foyer bock"; 19th century, Bavarian). Didn't like theology. Feuerbach believed that God is a human projection, which we create in our own image, thus concurring with the sentiment of the ancient Greek poet Xenophanes (Zenoffaneez"), who said that if horses and cows could draw, they would draw the gods looking like horses and cows. Feuerbach once indicated that his principal goal was to transform "the friends of God into friends of man, believers into thinkers, worshippers into workers, candidates for the other world into students of this world, Christians, who on their own confession are half-animal and half-angel, into men—whole men." Famous quote: "You are what you eat." Patron saint of health and diet books.

John Stuart Mill

JOHN STUART MILL (19th century, British). Famous proponent of Utilitarianism—in moral theory the belief that we always ought to act for the greatest happiness of the greatest number of people ("the greatest happiness principle"). By the age of 3, Mill had a reading knowledge of Latin; by the age of 8, a mastery of Greek; by the age of 11, a facility in mathematics; by the age of 21, a nervous breakdown. He once said: "It's better to be Socrates dissatisfied than a pig satisfied." Famous rejoinder: "Ask the pig." Mill was once arrested at the age of 17 for handing out birth control information in Hyde Park, a fact confusing to some of his followers, fellow utilitarians, who cannot figure out whether, in his infamous criminal act, he was ultimately attempting to promote the greatest happiness of the greatest number, or rather the greatest happiness of a lesser number.

Soren Kierkegaard

SOREN KIERKEGAARD ("Cur-ca-gore", or "Keer-ca-guard" - Americanized pronunciation; 19th century, Danish). A profound religious writer often publishing his work pseudonymously, Kierkegaard constantly made fun of the eminent philosopher Hegel. He was a great philosophical wit, as well as being the Father of Existentialism, a combination many people find surprising. The idea of "a leap of faith" was one of his best known contributions to religious thought. The importance of subjective engagement was another of his important themes. An inspired as well as an inspiring writer, he once wrote a 100 page book (*Philosophical Fragments*) and later published a postscript to it of over 500 pages (*Concluding Unscientific Postscript*). The twentieth century philosopher Wittgenstein, himself no existentialist, at one time expressed the opinion that Kierkegaard was the greatest thinker of his century, but added in criticism of his writing style: "He is too long-winded; he keeps on saying the same thing over and over again. When I read him I always wanted to say, 'Oh all right, I agree, I agree, but please get on with it.'" As an example of his views on philosophy, the following passage is typical:

"The difference between 'popular' and

'philosophical' is the amount of time a thing takes. Ask a man: do you know this or do you not know it—if he answers immediately, then the answer is popular, he is an undergraduate. If it takes ten years for the answer to come, and if it comes in the form of a system, if it is not quite clear whether he knows it or not, then it is a philosophical answer and the man a professor of philosophy—at least that is what he ought to be."

Lest it be thought that Kiekegaard favors the popular in all ways, his remarks on the most active purveyors of popular learning and taste should also be quoted: "God knows that I am not blood-thirsty and I think I have in a terrible degree a sense of my responsibility to God; but nevertheless, I should be ready to take the responsibility upon me, in God's name, of giving the order to fire if I could first of all make absolutely and conscientiously sure that there was not a single man standing in front of the rifles, not a single creature, who was not—a journalist. That is said of the class as a whole."

"There were philosophers even before Hegel who took it upon themselves to explain existence, history. And it is true of all such attempts that providence can only smile at them. Though perhaps it has not exactly roared with laughter at them..."

—Kierkegaard

Karl Marx

KARL MARX (19th century, German). Not one of the famous brothers. Marx was strongly influenced by Hegel, but became a materialist, not an idealist. Of course, materialism is just that philosophical view which some have characterized with the slogan "All that matters is matter, never mind the mind." It is distinctive of Marx's thought that he saw all of history developing toward you-know-what (hint: *not* Madison Avenue Free Market Republican Capitalism). Some have seen in Marxism the potential for true human liberation. More astute observers explain that in Capitalist societies, man exploits man, whereas in Marxist societies it is the other way around.

Charles Saunders Peirce

CHARLES SAUNDERS PEIRCE ("Purse", late 19th, early 20th century, American). Very smart, but had trouble getting a regular teaching position. This may be related to the fact that he reportedly made a habit of seducing colleagues' wives. He is also said to have run off with his French maid. Peirce was once arrested for running down the street and shouting philosophical paradoxes at innocent people. There are twenty boxes of his collected papers (essays) at Harvard; there would be more, but he was so poor at the end of his life that he burned his philosophical writings to stay warm on cold New England nights. There are many other philosophers whose works would have been more appropriately used for this purpose.

Friederich Nietzsche

FRIEDERICH NIETZSCHE ("Freed Rick Nee-chee"; 19th century, German). The ideal human = "the Overman" or "the Superman", the self-assured, aggressive individual who is a law unto himself. Typical quote: "I am not a man, I am dynamite." Autobiography title: *Ecce Homo* ("Behold, the Man," the famous statement used by Pontius Pilate in reference to Jesus). Its four chapter titles: "Why I Am So Wise," "Why I Am So Clever," "Why I Write Such Good Books," "Why I Am A Destiny." Nietzsche went insane from syphilis; he was found one day in the street, crazed and hanging onto the head of a horse—perhaps the first time in history that both ends of a horse have gotten together.

V.

Twentieth Century Philosophy

John Dewey

*J*OHN DEWEY (late 19th, early 20th century, American). Professor at Columbia University who believed that philosophy is coextensive with the whole human adventure. Dewey was one of the philosophers called "pragmatists". It is sometimes said that the central theme of his work can be summed up in the injunction "Don't argue, do something about it." Once, when he was working in his first floor study directly underneath the bathroom, he felt water dripping on the back of his neck. Dashing upstairs he was confronted with the sight of his little boy Freddie in an overflowing bathtub filled with toy boats. Unable to shut off the water, the small boy looked up at his father and said immediately, "Don't argue, John. Get the mop."

Bertrand Russell

BERTRAND RUSSELL (20th century [d. 1970], British). Renowned for work in logic and romantic escapades, he was a fertile thinker who changed his mind a lot and was enormously influential. Russell began to express his intense curiosity about the world from the time that he was three days old, as we know from his mother's writing then: "He lifts his head up and looks about in an energetic way." Told at the age of five that the world is round, he refused to believe it, but began digging a hole outdoors to see whether he would end up, bottom end up, in Australia. As it turns out, he didn't get to Australia until his late seventies. Early on, he became fascinated with mathematics, a study which awakened his philosophical interests. Later in life he once summed up his intellectual history by saying that when he became too stupid for mathematics he took to philosophy, and when he became too stupid for philosophy he turned to history. Russell did write on a wide variety of topics and often had quite interesting things to say: Democracy, for example, has at least one merit—elected officials cannot be more stupid than the electorate, for the more stupid the official is, the more stupid yet the people were to vote for him. Once asked by a publisher to write a complimentary foreword to a book by a philosopher whom Russell thought always stole his ideas, Russell replied: "Modesty forbids." In his late sixties, he was offered a position at the College of the City of New York, but because of a taxpayer's suit to anull the appointment initiated by a Brooklyn dentist's wife, he was legally ruled morally unfit to teach New Yorkers and was prevented from accepting such a position. In the suit, his books were described as "lecherous, salacious, libidinous, lustful, venerous, erotomaniac, aphrodisiac, atheistic, irreverent, narrow-minded, untruthful, and bereft of moral fibre." The philosopher Wittgenstein commented when he heard about this that if anything was the opposite of aphrodisiac it was Russell writing on sex. Russell predicted that only inhabitants of Tierra del Fuego (southern-most tip of South America) and, perhaps, a few Australians, would survive the next major war. He went on to win a Nobel Prize for Literature (because there isn't one for philosophy, and I want to know *why not?*).

Famous Russellian Proclamation:

"That Man is the product of causes which had no prevision of the end they were achieving; that his origin, his growth, his hopes and fears, his loves and his beliefs, are but the outcome of accidental collocations of atoms; that no fire, no heroism, no intensity of thought and feeling, can preserve an individual life beyond the grave; that all the labours of the ages, all the devotion, all the inspiration, all the noonday brightness of human genius, are destined to extinction in the vast death of the solar system, and that the whole temple of Man's achievement must inevitably be buried beneath the debris of a universe in ruins—all these things, if not quite beyond dispute, are yet so nearly certain, that no philosophy which rejects them can hope to stand. Only within the scaffolding of these truths, only on the firm foundation of unyielding despair, can the soul's habitation henceforth be safely built."

P.S. Have a nice day.

Ludwig Wittgenstein

LUDWIG WITTGENSTEIN (pronounced "Vittgenshtine", 20th century, [d. 1951]; Austrian born, taught at Cambridge). As a student of aeronautical engineering at Manchester, Wittgenstein became fascinated with philosophical problems concerning the foundations of mathematics, and so went to study with Russell at Cambridge. Immediately, the other famed Cambridge philosopher G.E. Moore formed a very high opinion of him. Asked why, Moore replied: "Because he's the only one who looks puzzled during my lectures." At the end of the first term, Wittgenstein asked Russell to tell him if he was a complete idiot, because if he was he would give up philosophy and go back to airplane design (a comforting thought for fliers!). Russell sent him to write a philosophical essay, read the first sentence and told him to stay in philosophy. Very soon he wrote a landmark book, the *Tractatus*, in which he claimed to have solved all the problems of philosophy, and with remarkable consistency left philosophy to become an elementary school teacher. Later he designed a mansion in Vienna and worked at other jobs, but he changed his mind about the *Tractatus* and returned to Cambridge to do philosophical work. An unbelievably intense and serious worker, he once said: "My father was a business man, and I am a business man: I want my philosophy to be business-like, to get something done, to get something settled." Intolerant of sloppiness and foolishness in others, he explained to a student, "A bad philosopher is like a slum landlord. It is my job to put him out of business." He was often quite blunt: At one discussion, another philosopher began to quote Kant in German, and Wittgenstein shouted at him to "*shut up*." This no-nonsense intensity took its toll: Wittgenstein became addicted to detective magazines and Hollywood movies, especially relishing Ginger Rogers and Fred Astaire. A tremendous amount of enormously influential work of his has been published since his death, in a number of difficult books, though he himself once said that a serious and good philosophical work could be written that would consist entirely of jokes.

"If this is nuts, don't be surprised, for so am I."

—Wittgenstein

Jean-Paul Sartre

J EAN-PAUL SARTRE ("Sart"; 20th century, French). Wrote a book called *Nausea*. Best known of the existentialists. Sartre first became excited about the philosophical approach known as phenomenology when, as he was having drinks with a friend, the man said, "You see, *mon petit comrad*, if you're a phenomenologist, you can talk about this drink, and it's philosophy," a remark anticipating, perhaps, something of the spirit of the more recent adage that philosophy is one of the only professions in which you can lie on the beach all day and tell people you're working. Often pictured with his pipe and a cup of coffee, Sartre was also an avid consumer of amphetamines, a speed freak. He is known to have written books under the influence, books whose individual sentences sometimes ramble on for more than a page. One recent biographer mentions a number of literary predecessors who likewise depended on chemical support and then comments that "What is odd about the case of Sartre is that though he wrote philosophy while stoned, he took care to keep his mental faculties intact while writing fiction," although how this commentator distinguishes between Sartre's philosophy and fiction, I must admit, escapes me. Sartre took a sensual delight in writing, turning out an estimated average of twenty pages a day. But many of his activities were frenetic. He paced the floor so much, he wore the rug threadbare in Simone de Beauvoir's apartment. In the midst of all this activity, he did sometimes come up with interesting ideas. For example, he once decided to explore "the metaphysics of boredom," and wrote "What is boredom? It is where there is simultaneously *too much* and *not enough*." Big book: *Being and Nothingness* (Doesn't leave out much). Famous quote: "Hell is other people." Not the life of the party.

Free Clip-n-Save Existentialist Mantra

Nothingness

Instructions: Xerox this page, clip the copy of the above, wallet-sized Existentialist Mantra, following the dotted lines, and paying particular attention to the empty spaces between the dots. To produce in yourself a genuine existentialist mood, stare at this mantra, reflect upon it, wallow in it. Best done on an empty stomach. Mantra card can be plasticized for greater permanence in this impermanent world.

Willard van Orman Quine

WILLARD VAN ORMAN QUINE (Rhymes with "Fine"; 20th century, American). Renowned Harvard philosopher and logician who was born in Akron, Ohio and who has travelled to all sorts of places on numerous, unusual forms of transportation: He has hitched rides across the country on the tops of freight trains, flown in a bomber and gone belly down on a surfboard in the Pacific Ocean, coached by fellow surfer and philosopher Donald Davidson. At one time in Mexico, an investigation into the meaning of a strange word culminated in his eating a noxious paste made of inch-long black bugs, an experience which haunted his digestive tract for days. Recounting it years later, he remarked, "Such are the rigors of semantics in the field." Quine found a title for one of his famous books when he was sitting in a Greenwich Village night spot hearing Harry Belafonte sing the last lines of a Trinidad calypso: "And so, *from a logical point of view*, Always marry woman uglier than you." Once expressed his perspective on ontology (questions of What there is, ultimately speaking) by comparison with his "preface for desert landscapes"—the philosophical equivalent of the aesthetic slogan "Less is More", more or less. Famous themes: "The radical indeterminacy of translation," "the inscrutability of reference." What do these phrases mean? Don't ask, unless you're prepared to leave the realm of casual bluffing far behind...

This is the end of our look at the philosophers, the thinkers who have given us philosophy, their lives and their ideas. Are there any more good stories about philosophers born after Quine? There are lots—interesting, insightful, funny, even hilarious stories in great numbers. And they can be heard at any of the annual meetings of the American Philosophical Association Convention, if you listen in on the right conversations.

APPENDIX :
Assorted, Often Remembered
Sayings and Questions

1. **"Know Thyself"** - Inscription on the oracle at Delphi.

2. **"Eureka"** - ("I have found it"), exclamation of Archimedes, an ancient Greek philosopher and mathematician, making a discovery in the bath tub.

3. **"What is Truth?"** - Pontius Pilate

4. **"Why is there Something rather than Nothing?"**
   - Famous cosmological question.

5. **"If a tree fell in the forest and nobody heard it fall, would it still make a noise?"**
   - Great conversational irritant.

6. **Philosophy?**
   "Unintelligible answers to insoluble problems."
   - Henry Adams
   "A philosopher is a blind man in a dark room looking for a black cat that isn't there."
   - Lord Bowen
   "A philosopher is one who contradicts other philosophers."
   - William James

"Philosophy is common sense in a dress suit."

> \- Oliver S. Braston

7. **"Metaphysics is the finding of bad reasons for what we believe on instinct."**
   - F.H. Bradley (famous metaphysician)

8. **"There is nothing so absurd but some philosopher has said it."**
   - Cicero (some philosopher)

9. **"To Be Is To Do."** - Thomist
   "To Do Is To Be." - Existentialist
   "Do Be Do Be Do." - Sinatra

THE BLUFFER'S BIBLIOGRAPHY

This is a brief listing of books which have been found especially useful by pretenders to philosophical knowledge. They are presented here in order of accessibility and usefulness in ordinary bluffing contexts. The last few volumes listed are for consultation in only the most demanding of bluff circumstances, in case, for example, you find yourself with room reservations for the hotel which will be housing the annual American Philosophical Association meetings, or if you should someday be invited to dine with a past or present graduate student in philosophy. Consultation of the more advanced volumes is to be limited to times of preparation for such extreme circumstances, else you risk a dangerous and nearly irreversible transition from bluffer to pundit.

1.   **Biographical Encyclopedia of Philosophy**
     Henry Thomas. Garden City, N.Y.:
     Doubleday and Company, Inc. 1965.

2.   **Bartlett's Familiar Quotations**
     Revised and Enlarged Edition.
     John Bartlett. Boston:
     Little, Brown and Company, 1980.

3.   **A Dictionary of Philosophy**
     Antony Flew. New York:
     St. Martin's Press, 1979

4.   **A History of Western Philosophy**
     Bertrand Russell.   New York:
     Simon and Schuster, 1945

5.   **Dictionary of Philosophy and Religion:**
     Eastern and Western Thought
     William L. Reese
     Atlantic Highlands, N.J.:
     Humanities Press, 1980

6.   **A New History of Philosophy**
     2 volumes
     Wallace I. Matson.   New York:
     Harcourt Brace Jovanovich, 1987

7.   **The Encyclopedia of Philosophy**
     8 Big volumes
     Edited by Paul Edwards.   New York:
     Macmillan Publishing Co., Inc. and
     The Free Press, 1967

8.   **A History of Philosophy**
     Lots and Lots of paperback volumes.
     Frederick Copleston.   New York:
     Doubleday, 1962

     The source most widely used by graduate
     students in preparation for exams (al-
     though they, of course—bluffers that they
     are—want their professors to think they
     have read the original sources).